Institutional Trading

Ricardo Moreno

AF721965

Copyright Page

Copyright Holder: © Ricardo Moreno
Author: © Ricardo Moreno 2025
Publisher: Flamenco
Release Year 2025
All Rights Reserved

All text, illustrations, photographs, graphics, logos, and other content included in this book are the exclusive property of the author and are protected by national and international intellectual property laws. Reproduction, distribution, public communication, transformation, or any other form of exploitation of all or part of this work is strictly prohibited without the prior express written permission of the author.

Index

The Mind of the Institutional Trader

Most traders start out believing that trading is just a matter of technique: finding the right strategy, following a few rules, and making money. But those who manage to trade like true professionals understand that success lies not only in what you do, but in how you think. The mind of an institutional trader works completely differently than that of a beginner or even an intermediate trader. It's not just about trading, but about trading with a business acumen, with structure, with calm, with absolute control over your emotions, and with a strategic clarity that doesn't waver with the market.

An institutional trader isn't driven by impulses. He knows that every decision has consequences. He's not thinking about getting rich tomorrow, or doubling his account this week, or predicting the next big gain. He thinks like a surgeon. He analyzes, waits, executes, and repeats. For him, every trade is just another part of the process, not a lottery ticket. His focus isn't on immediate profit, but on long-term consistency. His goal isn't just to make money, but to do so in a sustainable, replicable, and structured way.

This type of trader understands that the market is unpredictable, but he also knows that he can be predictable within himself. He works to master his behavior, not the market. He knows that the key to success lies in controlling his mind, his emotions, and his impulses. While most stress when the price goes against them, he breathes and follows his plan. While others get excited when they win, he evaluates whether what he did was right or just luck. He constantly judges his decisions, not by the outcome, but by the quality of the process he followed.

An institutional mind doesn't react to the market; it responds intelligently. It knows there are days to trade and days to wait. It doesn't feel anxious if it doesn't enter a trade. It has patience because it has understood that money lies in waiting, in precision, in quality, not in quantity. Many traders fail because they seek constant action. They trade out of boredom, anxiety, or fear of missing out. The institutional trader trades only when they have an objective reason to do so.

Another crucial aspect is that the institutional trader isn't obsessed with being right. For them, being wrong is part of the game. The important thing isn't always being right, but rather managing errors well. They lose gracefully, knowing that a controlled loss isn't a threat, but an operating cost. They don't chase the market, they don't retaliate, they don't trade out of frustration. When they lose, they evaluate and learn. When they win, they evaluate and reinforce what's right. Their learning is constant, not just when something goes wrong.

Institutional traders also think as a team, even if they initially operate alone. They know that success on a large scale isn't achieved alone. They think about processes, systems, and how to scale what they do. They don't want to be just a good trader; they want to build a structure that can function with or without them at the helm. This forces them to think with a leader's mindset. They demand higher standards of themselves. They don't allow themselves to improvise. They have clear routines, hours of analysis, defined times for trading, and times to review their mistakes.

On an emotional level, the institutional trader works on his maturity. He doesn't seek strong emotions. He doesn't crave adrenaline. In fact, his days are often boring, monotonous, and disciplined. That's what makes him a professional. While others need excitement to feel alive in trading, he seeks stability. He knows that exaggerated emotions are dangerous, both euphoria and despair. He has understood that inner peace is a competitive advantage.

Finally, the institutional trader's mind doesn't depend on motivation. It depends on discipline. He doesn't need inspiration to do what he has to do. He has systems that guide him. He's turned his habits into his shield. He gets up, analyzes, reviews, trades if necessary, records everything, corrects what needs correcting, and moves forward. He doesn't dramatize. He doesn't procrastinate. He doesn't make excuses. He understands that trading is a serious business, not a game, and he acts accordingly.

When you manage to think like this, you transform. You're no longer just another trader. You're a professional who approaches the market with the respect, composure, and strategy of someone who understands that this business isn't about beating the market, but about beating yourself every day. And when that happens, what you build stops depending on luck and starts depending on your character. That's the true mind of the institutional trader.

Professional Trading Infrastructure

If you want to operate like an institutional trader, you can't rely on an old laptop and an unstable Wi-Fi connection at the corner cafe. This isn't a hobby. It's a business, and like any serious business, it requires professional infrastructure. In the world of trading, infrastructure is what separates those who play from those who win. Having the right tools not only improves your results but also allows you to make decisions quickly, accurately, and with confidence. You can't afford to trade with technical uncertainty. Every second counts, every click matters, and every mistake can cost you money.

It all starts with the hardware. Most institutional traders work with powerful computers. This doesn't mean you need a supercomputer, but you do need a fast machine with a good processor, plenty of RAM (minimum 16GB), and, if possible, more than one screen. The reason for having multiple screens isn't for luxury or appearance, but because you need to view multiple charts, platforms, news, economic data, and tools at the same time. Having everything on a single screen forces you to constantly switch between windows, which reduces your reaction time. And in trading, speed is money.

Internet connection is also critical. You need a wired connection, not Wi-Fi, preferably with high speed and low latency. This means your orders will be executed more quickly and reliably. A half-second delay can make the difference between winning or losing at certain times. Many advanced traders even hire secondary connections as backups or use VPS servers (virtual private servers) located near the broker's server to further minimize latency. This is especially useful if you work with automated systems or algorithmic trading.

Next comes the trading platform. Not all are created equal. Some brokers offer basic platforms, while others have professional platforms with advanced features. You need a platform that's stable, customizable, offers good order execution, real-time charts, and technical analysis tools. Some of the most popular in the institutional world are MetaTrader 5, NinjaTrader, TradingView (for analysis), or proprietary platforms from institutional brokers like Interactive Brokers, Thinkorswim, or cTrader. The key is that you feel comfortable using it, that it's efficient, and that it allows you to trade without technical errors.

At the same time, you must have a reliable source of financial data. Many novice traders use free data, but it often suffers from delays or lower quality. At the institutional level, services such as Bloomberg Terminal, Reuters, or premium real-time market data feeds are used. This is especially important if you trade assets where price changes are rapid, and any information advantage can make a difference. Having real-time data, without delays or errors, gives you a huge advantage over those who are trading "blind" or with outdated information.

You should also have analytical tools that go beyond basic charting. This includes backtesting software to historically test strategies, statistical programs to evaluate your performance, and even spreadsheets or custom systems to record all your trades and key metrics. You can't improve what you don't measure. An institutional trader has their numbers straight: win ratio, maximum drawdown, winning percentage, average profit per trade, and more. All of this is monitored and analyzed. It's a data culture.

As your operation grows, you also need to protect your information. Cybersecurity isn't optional. Having strong passwords, two-factor authentication, constant backups of your data, and recovery systems in case of technical failures are part of the job. The worst time to realize you didn't back up is when your computer crashes in the middle of an ongoing operation Professionals prevent, they don't improvise.

Another essential component is the broker. This is where many fail. Not all brokers are created equal. An institutional trader doesn't trade with little-known, unregulated brokers or brokers with huge spreads. You need a reliable, regulated broker with good execution, low latency, direct market access, and competitive commissions. Sometimes, paying a small commission is better if it means better execution and greater transparency. Many advanced traders even work with ECN brokers, which connect them directly to liquidity providers, eliminating intermediaries.

In addition to the technical aspects, there's a less visible but equally important aspect: the environment. You can't operate in chaos. You need an orderly, quiet, comfortable workspace where you can focus. This may seem minor, but your environment directly influences your mental performance. A comfortable chair, good lighting, clean air, and the absence of distractions make the difference between trading clearly or making errors due to stress or fatigue. Institutional trading is an intense mental activity, and you need to be physically and mentally prepared.

Finally, you must have access to information that isn't just technical. Many professional traders have real-time financial news services, economic alerts, and even advisors to help them interpret certain market events. Information is valuable. Not for predicting the future, but for understanding the context. Knowing what events are happening, how they might affect the assets you trade, and how to anticipate certain big moves is part of the job. It's not just about seeing candles on a chart; it's about seeing the bigger picture.

All this infrastructure isn't built overnight, but it's important to know where you're headed. Each component you add should bring you closer to a more professional, more precise, and more profitable trade. You don't need to spend thousands of dollars from day one, but you do need to have a clear plan for evolution. Ask yourself: What do I need to trade better? What part of my technical system is weak? What should I improve now, and what can I scale later? That's thinking like an institutional trader. That's the mindset that prepares you not only to trade well, but to build a real trading business—one that's solid, professional, and ready to grow.

Profitable and Scalable Trading Models

A professional trader doesn't just think about how to make money today; they also think about how to make their trading model profitable and scalable over time. This means they aren't satisfied with trading well for a few weeks; they seek to create a system that can grow, multiply, be automated, or even be taught to others to generate passive income. It's not enough to know how to enter and exit the market; you have to build trading models that function like a business. They must have structure, repeatability, risk control, and, above all, they must not depend solely on the trader's mood or luck at the right moment.

To begin, you need to understand what makes a trading model profitable. Profitability doesn't just mean making a lot of money; it means winning consistently. A profitable model has a clear strategy, defined rules, a logical approach, and, above all, strict risk management. If your model can survive difficult months, remain stable during different market conditions, and continue to produce profits over the long term, then it's a profitable model. It doesn't matter if you make ten trades a month or a hundred; if your results are positive, stable, and repeatable, you're on the right track.

But profitability isn't everything. If your model only works when you're in charge, if you need to spend eight hours a day monitoring the market, if everything depends on your energy, your mood, and your availability, then that model isn't scalable. To scale a trading model, you need it to work without you or with less intervention from you. This can be achieved in different ways: by automating parts of the process, creating a team to operate your strategy, or teaching your system to others to execute in exchange for a commission or shared profit.

One of the most common and scalable models is algorithmic trading. Here you design a clear strategy and program it into a system that executes trades automatically. It requires no emotions, no distractions, and can even trade while you sleep. This model requires technical knowledge and extensive testing, but once it works, it's highly scalable. You can run it on multiple instruments, with different accounts, at different times. You can even sell the algorithm or charge for its use. It's a model that not only generates income, it also frees up your time.

Another scalable model is to create a trading room. This involves bringing together several traders who operate under the same strategy, with supervision and discipline. You can be the leader, the creator of the system, and the others execute it. You earn a portion of their profits or charge a fee for being part of the team. If your strategy is good and you have the ability to teach, this model can grow quickly. It also allows you to diversify your risk: you no longer depend solely on your account, but on the collective performance.

You can also turn your model into a training system. If your strategy works and you have verifiable results, you can teach others how to replicate it. Courses, mentorships, memberships, online academies. This not only generates additional income, but also forces you to professionalize your system. No one pays to learn something messy. If your model is clear, measurable, and can be taught step by step, then you have a gold mine in your hands. The best part is that you can scale it without limits: a video can be taught thousands of times without having to repeat anything.

Some traders also scale their model by becoming money managers. This means others give you their money to trade under your system. You charge a commission based on performance or a fixed management fee. The key here is trust and results. No one hands over their money to just anyone. But if you manage to build a solid, transparent, and professional track record, this model can allow you to manage large volumes of money without having to risk only your own capital. It's scalable because you can have many investors following a single centralized strategy.

Now, for any of these models to work, your strategy must meet a few requirements. First, it must be simple. Complex strategies often fail when market conditions change. Second, it must be measurable. You need to know how much you win on average, how much you lose, what your success rate is, and how far you can fall at your worst.

Without this data, you can't project, scale, or improve. Third, it must be replicable. If only you can execute it, then you are limited. A good strategy can be taught, automated, or clearly guided to others.

It's also important that your model has a constant review process. Markets change, and models must also be adjusted. An institutional trader isn't wedded to a fixed idea. They hold weekly meetings to review results, adjust parameters, identify errors, and optimize the system. This culture of continuous improvement is what allows the model to remain profitable and grow over time. A stagnant system is doomed to die. A living, flexible, and adaptable model has a future.

A common misconception is that scaling is simply about doubling your capital. That's not the case. Scaling is multiplying the reach of your model. You can scale capital, but also personnel, technology, and impact. You can operate with more accounts, in more markets, with more people, and with more schedules. The important thing is that the model remains firm in its essence: profitable, controlled, and with logic behind it. There's no point in growing if you can't sustain it.

In short, a profitable and scalable trading model is one that generates consistent profits and can grow without relying solely on you. Whether through automation, teamwork, training, or capital management, the important thing is to build something with structure and a vision for the future. If you achieve that, then you will not only be a successful trader, but the creator of a true money-making machine. A machine that can work regardless of whether you're in front of the screen or not. That's the goal of every institutional trader: to stop being an operator and become a builder of systems that work, grow, and change lives.

Regulation and Legality of Institutional Trading

When you start trading as an independent trader, it's easy to overlook the legal aspect. You open an account, make a few trades, make or lose money, and move on without giving much thought to the formalities. But when you decide to grow and move into the world of institutional trading, the story changes completely. It's no longer just about you and your personal account. It's about managing third-party money, building a team, possibly opening a company, and operating with the seriousness that the financial system requires. And at that point, understanding regulations and legality becomes mandatory, not optional.

The first step is to understand that each country has its own laws regarding trading, investment, and capital management. You can't simply accept other people's money to trade and keep a portion of the profits without being regulated. Doing so without licenses can lead to serious problems: from fines to criminal penalties. Therefore, if your business model includes managing third-party funds or teaching trading on a large scale, you need to know what regulations apply in your country and how to comply with them.

In most countries, if you manage other people's money, you need to register as a financial advisor or investment manager with the appropriate regulatory body. For example, in the United States, there is the SEC (Securities and Exchange Commission) and FINRA. In Europe, there are different regulators per country, such as the CNMV in Spain, BaFin in Germany, and the FCA in the United Kingdom. Similar bodies also exist in Latin America: the National Banking and Securities Commission in Mexico, the Superintendency of the Securities Market in Peru, and the CVM in Brazil, among others. If you are not regulated, you cannot legally offer investment services, much less advertise them.

Now, do you need a license if you only trade your own capital? No, in most cases you don't. If you're only trading your own money, there's no legal issue. But the moment you start managing money from family, friends, or external investors, or when you decide to create an agency or trading company, the story changes. Although many people trade other people's funds without licenses, that doesn't mean it's allowed or even smart to do so. You're building a business, and a serious business is built with clear rules from the start.

A common legal option is to establish a formal business. You can create a legally incorporated company, register your activity as an investment business, and hire a lawyer to help you with the appropriate legal framework. This will allow you to invoice services, sign management contracts, and, above all, protect yourself legally. Many traders create legal structures such as limited liability companies or corporations to separate their personal assets from their business assets. This also allows them to operate with greater confidence and transparency for their clients.

Another option is to partner with a regulated company. Instead of creating everything from scratch, you can seek to work under the legal umbrella of an already licensed firm. For example, some prop trading or asset management firms allow independent traders to operate under their supervision, respecting their internal policies and compliance standards. This option is useful if you're not yet ready to pay the costs of full regulation on your own, but still want to operate professionally and legally.

Don't forget the tax issue. The money you generate from trading, whether your own or through third parties, has tax implications. You must declare your income, pay the corresponding taxes, and keep organized accounting records. Many traders ignore this at first, but when they start earning significant amounts, they realize that not having everything in order can become a major headache. It's best to work with an accountant or tax advisor who understands trading and can help you meet your obligations without overpaying or underpaying.

Additionally, when you have a team or form an agency, labor laws, contracts, data protection, intellectual property, and many other issues come into play that may seem unrelated to trading but are part of the legal ecosystem of any business. If you sell courses or training, you need terms and conditions, return policies, and possibly intellectual property registrations. If you manage databases with customer information, you must comply with data protection laws such as the GDPR in Europe or the Habeas Data Law in several Latin American countries. All of this is part of running a real institutional operation.

Many traders make the mistake of thinking this level of formality is unnecessary or can wait. But in reality, the sooner you understand the rules of the game, the faster you can grow without fear. Large companies aren't afraid of being investigated because they know they're doing things right. That gives them an advantage. Operating with peace of mind, knowing that your contracts are well-written, that your clients are protected, and that your income is properly declared, allows you to focus on what's most important: operating and growing.

The world of institutional trading is not a rule-free realm. It's a financial business, and as such, it's regulated. Understanding this from the outset positions you as a professional. It gives you credibility with your clients, trust with your partners, and security against any audit or inspection. Furthermore, when the time comes to scale, raise capital, or sell your company, having everything legally in order will be one of your greatest strengths.

In short, if you want to build a serious business in the trading world, you need to understand and respect regulations. Whether you manage funds, teach, automate, build a team, or sell your system, there are laws that apply to you. Don't wait until you have a problem to learn them. Get informed, seek advice, and build your operation on solid foundations. Legality isn't an obstacle; it's a springboard. And it's one of the main reasons why true institutional traders manage to stand out from the rest and endure over time.

Selection of Traders

Selecting traders for your team isn't simply about finding people who know how to push buttons and read charts. It's one of the most important decisions you'll make if you want to build a truly successful institutional trading team. A bad trader can waste your money, time, reputation, and energy. On the other hand, a good trader, well chosen, can become one of your organization's most valuable assets. Therefore, it's not about filling chairs; it's about finding the right people for a very specific mission: making money work for you intelligently, methodically, and profitably.

The first thing you need to understand is that you're not looking for market geniuses. Geniuses tend to be difficult to manage; they don't follow rules, believe they're above the system, and often end up doing crazy things with other people's money. You need people who are disciplined, patient, responsible, and, above all, trainable. The best institutional trader isn't the brightest, but the most consistent. The one who can repeat a pattern without deviating, the one who is comfortable trading under pressure without losing their cool, and the one who understands that success in this business comes more from repetition and self-control than from intuition.

Before accepting someone onto your team, you need to look at three main areas: mindset, technical skill, and teamwork. Mindset is the first thing you should assess. Is this person emotionally self-controlled? Can they follow instructions without arguing every step of the way? Can they lose without collapsing? Can they win without becoming arrogant? You can measure this in interviews, but also with small practical challenges. Give them a fictitious capital for a week and observe how they react to a losing streak. See if they stick to the plan. If they can't stick to a practice plan, they'll never stick to a real one.

Then comes the technical part. It doesn't matter whether they trade stocks, futures, or forex. What matters is that they understand the fundamentals of the analysis you use in your business. Do you use price action? Algorithmic strategies? Statistical models? Not all traders are compatible with all styles. A scalper can be a disaster in a swing or institutional environment. That's why it's best to look for people with a solid foundation but flexible in their trading style, who can adapt to your methodology. Even if someone doesn't have much experience but shows an ability to learn quickly and understand your system, they can be more valuable than someone with years of experience who doesn't adapt.

Many traders have good results in their personal accounts, but when you put them in a structured environment, with clear rules and allocated capital, they fail. This is because they're not used to working under real pressure or following an external methodology. You don't need improvisers; you need systematic traders. That's why, once someone passes the initial screening, it's key to run real tests. Assign them a demo account with a predefined system, ask them to document each trade, and analyze whether they adhere to the process. You're not looking for occasional winners; you're looking for market soldiers.

The third area is the ability to integrate into a team. An institutional trader doesn't work alone. They have to coordinate with others, communicate their decisions, participate in review meetings, and be open to feedback. This is where many fail. If someone has a inflated ego, doesn't accept criticism, or withdraws into their own world, they will be a burden on the team. On the other hand, someone who knows how to collaborate, share ideas, and build alongside others will help you create a strong culture. You don't need stars; you need professional-minded team players.

In practice, you can design a selection process in stages. First, an interview to understand their motivation and experience. Then, a theoretical test to validate their basic knowledge. Then, a simulation with a demo account for one or two weeks, where results and behavior are evaluated. Finally, a gradual integration into the team with reduced capital, to see how they perform in a real environment. This process may seem lengthy, but it will prevent serious problems later.

Another important aspect is to clearly define what you're looking for from the start. Do you need operational traders to run your system? Analysts to develop ideas for the team? Mentors to train new members? Not everyone fits every role. If you select wisely from the start, you'll have less turnover, less frustration, and better results.

It's also key to establish a continuous evaluation system. It's not enough to simply select well. Performance must be reviewed regularly. You can have clear metrics: percentage of plan fulfillment, consistency of results, level of risk taken, contributions to the team, etc. This allows for constant feedback and maintains high quality. If someone's performance drops, it's quickly noticed. If someone improves, it's also noticeable. This creates a culture of constant improvement and individual accountability within a collective framework.

And finally, don't forget something fundamental: select people who share your vision. People who want to grow with you, who understand where your trading agency is going, and who feel part of something bigger than just an account. Money is important, of course. But if you only hire people who are there for the money, they'll leave at the first stumble. On the other hand, if you build a team that believes in the project, that values learning, growth, and collaborative development, you'll be creating a truly institutional organization with a future.

Selecting traders is like choosing the pillars of a building. If you choose well, your structure will be strong and durable. If you choose poorly, it will collapse at the first strong wind of the market. Don't rush. Evaluate carefully. Listen beyond the words. See what they do, not just what they say. And always remember that you're not looking for solitary traders; you're looking for partners on a serious mission: to build a professional, stable, and scalable trading machine. That selection, when done well, is the first step to making everything else work.

Train to Win

Training a trader isn't simply teaching them how to use a platform or explaining how an indicator works. Training to win means shaping a person's mind, habits, vision, and discipline so they can trade the markets with clarity, control, and profitability. It's a process that goes far beyond technical knowledge. It involves a profound transformation that takes time, consistency, and a lot of patience. A successful institutional trader isn't born, it's built. And training is the foundation of that development.

When you decide to create an institutional trading team, you have to assume that you're going to be a coach in addition to a leader. You'll have to teach not only what to do, but how to think. And the first thing you must teach is the right mindset. Most people who come into trading do so with misconceptions: they believe it's about making a quick buck, that it's all a matter of luck, or finding "the perfect strategy." And that's not the case. The reality is that profitable trading is based on probabilities, repetition, risk management, and emotional mastery. Therefore, the first step in training must be to break all these myths and teach the truth about institutional trading: it's not about guessing, it's about executing well.

Effective training begins with a clear structure. You can't teach in a haphazard way. You need a training plan divided into stages, each with objectives, tools, and exercises. A good way to structure it is by levels. In the first level, you introduce the basic concepts: how the market works, what a trade is, what types of orders exist, how to read a candle, what a stop loss is, and how the risk-reward relationship works. Here, you're not looking for a perfect understanding of everything, just a solid foundation.

In the second level, the focus shifts to analysis. Here, you learn how to read the market, how to identify patterns, how to use indicators logically (without relying on them), and how to understand price behavior. The goal of this stage is for the trader to be able to analyze the market without feeling lost. It's not about predicting the future, but rather understanding what the market is showing right now.

At the third level, you move on to execution. Here, traders must learn how to build a trade from scratch: when to enter, where to place the stop, how to calculate position size, and when to exit. The most important thing at this stage is that they follow a plan. You can give them a system that works and ask them to repeat it over and over again. At first, it doesn't matter so much whether they win or lose; the important thing is that they do it well, with discipline. Because if they can follow a system in a demo, they can do it in real life.

Then comes the most difficult level: emotional management. This is where many fail. A trader can know everything technical, but if they don't control their emotions, they're lost. That's why you must train them to lose gracefully, to win with humility, to not overtrade, to not retaliate against the market, to not be afraid when the trade goes well. Emotional review exercises are very useful here, where the trader writes down how they felt on each trade, what they thought before entering, and how they reacted to the outcome. It's also very helpful to have feedback sessions where their decisions are analyzed, not just their results. Because making money doesn't always mean doing things right, and losing doesn't always mean doing things wrong either.

Throughout training, constant practice is essential. A trader trains like an athlete. They can't read a book and then expect to be profitable. They have to practice every day, repeat trades, analyze charts, take notes, and correct mistakes. That's why it's helpful to have simulations, weekly challenges, and performance reviews. You can assign specific tasks: for example, "This week you'll only look for range breakouts" or "This week you'll only trade with the trend." This forces them to focus, dig deeper, and develop real skills.

It's also vital to teach traders to think in terms of process, not results. Many get frustrated if they lose a trade, even if they did it well. Or they get excited if they win, even if it was a poorly executed trade. Real training involves separating execution from the result. If they did it right, even if they lost, that's a victory. If they won but did it poorly, that's a defeat. Teaching this way of thinking is one of the keys to long-term success.

One aspect that's often forgotten in training is documentation. A well-trained trader knows how to keep a trading journal. They write down every entry, every exit, every emotion, every mistake. They review their statistics. They identify behavioral patterns. This habit is one of the most powerful because it turns every experience into a lesson. And that's the true secret to growth: learning from every session.

It's also advisable to have a group feedback system. Once a week, you can hold a meeting with the entire team to review operations, share lessons learned, and discuss mistakes. It's not about criticizing, but about learning together. This not only improves the group's technical level but also strengthens team culture. No one feels alone. Everyone knows they're in a process and can count on each other's support.

Training to win also involves knowing when to push and when to release. Some traders need more pressure to stay focused. Others need confidence to stay focused. As a leader, your job is to get to know each member of your team and tailor your training to their profile. But always with the same goal: developing solid, stable, profitable traders.

Finally, good training never ends. Even the most advanced traders must continue learning. The market changes, conditions vary, and emotional challenges evolve. That's why maintaining a culture of continuous improvement is essential. You can do this with monthly workshops, analyzing new strategies, reading books, hosting special guests—anything that keeps knowledge alive.

Coaching to win isn't just about teaching trading; it's about developing mindsets, building habits, strengthening confidence, and preparing every team member to perform at their best when they're in the markets. And when you achieve that, you won't just have traders who make money. You'll have an institutional machine capable of producing sustainable results, day after day, without relying on luck or impulse. That's coaching to win. And that's the foundation of every great trading empire.

High Performance Culture in the Team

Creating a high-performance culture in an institutional trading team isn't simply about demanding results or imposing constant pressure. It goes far beyond that. It's about building an environment where all team members are committed to excellence, where discipline is part of everyday life, and where everyone is crystal clear that individual and collective growth is a top priority. It's a culture based on values, behaviors, and mindset. And most importantly, it's not imposed; it's built by example, repetition, and the right leadership.

A high-performance team isn't just a group of talented people working together. It's a perfectly coordinated system of growth-minded individuals with clear goals, solid routines, and an unwavering commitment to constant improvement. To achieve that, the first thing you need is clarity. Your team must know exactly what is expected of them. There can be no ambiguity. Every trader must understand the team's goals, what behavior is rewarded, the rules of the game, and how success is measured. This clarity prevents confusion and creates a solid foundation for focused trading.

The second pillar is discipline. Without discipline, there is no consistency, and without consistency, there are no sustainable results. This means arriving on time, following analysis routines, following the trading plan without deviation, conducting daily reviews, recording all trades, reviewing errors, and taking care of your physical and mental health. Every detail counts. In a high-performance team, no one does the bare minimum. Everyone does what they need to, even when they don't feel like it. Even when no one is looking. That's true discipline, and it's contagious. If you, as a leader, lead by example, your traders will do the same.

Another fundamental aspect is constant feedback. You can't build an elite team if you're not willing to correct what's wrong. But you also need to know how to do it. Good feedback doesn't humiliate or punish. It teaches, corrects, and improves. Every week, review the team's operations, analyze the most important decisions, identify repetitive errors, and offer specific solutions. Also, celebrate what's done well. When a trader makes a good decision even if they've lost, you should acknowledge it. This teaches them to value the process over the outcome. And that, in the long run, builds strong traders.

In addition to correcting mistakes, you must also reward good behavior. Not just with money or bonuses, but with recognition, with growth within the team, with more responsibilities. Recognition well applied is a very powerful fuel. It makes members feel valued, and wants to give more. On the other hand, when behaviors don't align with the team culture, you must act immediately. You can't allow negative attitudes, disorganization, irresponsibility, or inflated egos. A high-performance culture doesn't tolerate mediocre behavior. If you do, you're sending a message: that you can underperform here without consequences. And that kills any culture.

It's also key to foster a sense of belonging. People perform better when they feel they're part of something important. Therefore, you must build an environment where the team feels like a professional family. Do group activities, share achievements, establish internal symbols, and create rituals. All of this strengthens the bond between members and makes them work not only for themselves but also for others. A trader who feels part of a solid team doesn't want to fail. They don't want to disappoint. They want to add value and give their best.

Transparency is another vital factor. In a high-performance team, there are no secrets or mind games. If there's a problem, it's discussed. If someone is underperforming, it's analyzed with data. If there are changes in management, they're explained. This builds trust. And where there's trust, there's openness. Where there's openness, there's improvement. It's also important that everyone has access to performance metrics. Every trader should know how things are going, what they're doing well, what they need to correct, and how they compare to others—not to compete toxically, but to raise the overall bar.

Continuous learning is also an essential part of this culture. The best teams are always learning something new. They don't settle. They study new strategies, analyze major operations from the past, invite experts, read books, and run simulations. This keeps their minds active, their competitive spirit healthy, and their motivation ignite. You can't allow your team to enter their comfort zone. They must always be one step beyond what they already know.

Finally, a high-performance culture is sustained by leadership. You, as a leader, must be the first to lead by example. You must demonstrate discipline, self-control, focus, humility to learn, and firmness in making difficult decisions. Your behavior defines the team's standards. If you relax, they will too. If you raise the bar, they will want to catch up.

Building this culture isn't easy. It requires time, consistency, and many conversations. But once established, it becomes an advantage that's impossible to copy. Because while other teams struggle with mediocrity, yours soars with precision, focus, and drive. And it shows in the results, in the mindset, in the energy you breathe every day.

A high-performance culture isn't just a way of working. It's a way of experiencing trading. And it's the only way to build something truly great, solid, and lasting in this business. An institutional agency isn't built with good intentions; it's built with an extraordinary team. And that team only emerges when the culture is non-negotiable. When commitment is palpable. When every trader wants to be the best, not out of ego, but through excellence. Because they know that if they grow, the team grows. And if the team grows, the empire expands.

Key Roles Within the Trading Team

When forming a serious institutional trading team, it's not just about putting several traders together and putting them to work. It's about structuring a system where each person fulfills a specific role, has clear responsibilities, and knows how to contribute value to the common goal: generating profits in a consistent, scalable, and professional manner. A successful trading team is more like an orchestra than a group of soloists. Each member plays their own instrument, but everyone follows the same sheet music. Harmony is only achieved when everyone fully understands what they are supposed to do.

The most obvious role within the team is that of the operational trader. This person executes market trades, follows defined strategies, analyzes charts, makes real-time decisions, and manages their risk precisely. But not all traders operate the same. Some specialize in scalping, others in swing trading, others in algorithmic trading. Even within the team, there may be traders who only trade certain assets, such as currencies, futures, stocks, or cryptocurrencies. That's why it's important to clearly define each trader's strengths and align them with an overall strategy. It's not about everyone trading the same thing, but rather about each trader trading what they're proficient at, within the parameters of the team's system.

Then there's the market strategist. This person doesn't necessarily trade daily, but they're crucial to the team. They're responsible for analyzing the global economic context, news, macro data, and institutional behavior patterns. Based on all of this, they suggest adjustments, prepare weekly plans, and anticipate scenarios. Their work helps everyone trade with more context, understand why the market moves the way it does, and prepare more robust strategies. This role is also key to avoiding impulsive trades based solely on charts without understanding the underlying issues.

Another essential role is that of the risk manager. This team member isn't focused on making money, but rather on ensuring the team doesn't lose it irresponsibly. Their job is to set loss limits for each day, week, or month, control portfolio exposure, limit correlation between positions, and maintain capital stability. They are the ones who say this is the end of trading today if there has already been a large loss. Although this role can sometimes cause friction with traders who want to continue trading, their function is vital to the team's survival and sustainability. Well-managed risk is what keeps a trading firm alive.

There should also be someone who serves as an internal trainer or mentor. This role becomes more important as the team grows. They coach new traders, review their mistakes, provide personalized feedback, and help them accelerate their learning curve. Not all good traders know how to teach, so this role should fall to someone with pedagogical skills, patience, and strategic vision. If you train newcomers well, your team not only grows in number, but also in quality. And that's a huge advantage.

In more structured teams, there's also a systems programmer or algorithm developer. This person doesn't operate directly, but builds tools for traders. They range from automated execution systems to custom indicators, alerts, dashboards, news analysis bots, backtesters, and more. Their work helps traders save time, make better decisions, and increase their efficiency. A good institutional trading team always has someone who understands code, automation, and technology. They're part of the future of trading.

The performance analyst also plays a very important role. This member is responsible for reviewing the statistics of each trader, each strategy, and the team as a whole. They measure risk-reward ratios, win rates, drawdowns, trade duration, and performance by asset, day, and hour. Their analysis helps uncover what's working and what's not. It helps make decisions such as eliminating a strategy, adjusting a rule, or doubling capital in a system that's performing well. Without data, trading becomes a dangerous intuition. With data, it becomes a science.

The team coordinator or leader is the one who maintains the overall vision. Their job is to lead, make difficult decisions, resolve internal conflicts, maintain motivation, and align everyone with the goals. They set the pace, provide direction, and ensure each role is fulfilled correctly. They don't need to be the best trader in the group, but they do need to be the most reliable, clearest, and most committed. Their leadership defines the team's culture, and that makes the difference between a group that grows and one that stagnates.

As you grow, you can even include other roles such as talent recruiter, investor relations manager, or academy manager if you decide to teach others. These roles aren't operational, but they're key to scaling the model and turning it into an institutional agency that not only manages capital, but also trains traders, manages third-party funds, creates financial products, and generates diversified revenue.

Understanding that institutional trading is a structured business is what allows you to scale it. When you view traders only as trade executors, you miss the opportunity to build something big. But when you understand that a well-equipped team works like a machine where every part is vital, you begin to design with intention, hire intelligently, measure accurately, and grow with strategy. At that moment, you stop being an individual trader and become an empire builder. And that, without a doubt, is the most ambitious step you can take in the world of trading.

Scale Your Operation

Scaling an institutional trading operation isn't just about making more money. It's about transforming a profitable system into a solid, replicable structure capable of growing without losing control or quality. It's about moving from a functioning team to a dominant organization. Scaling means multiplying results without multiplying errors, and that requires method, clarity, and discipline.

The first step to scaling your operation is to have a strong foundation. You can't scale something that doesn't work consistently. If your team has unstable results, if every month is a roulette wheel, if your traders don't yet have solid processes, the worst thing you can do is add more capital or more people. That will only multiply the errors. Scaling doesn't begin with growth, it begins with stabilization. You need to verify that the system you're using produces predictable profits, with controlled risks, and without depending on luck or a whim of the day.

Once you have that solid foundation, the next step is to document absolutely everything. And when I say everything, I mean strategies, schedules, patterns, entry and exit criteria, risk management, analysis routines, error correction procedures, performance metrics, and reporting formats. Scalable institutional trading works like a high-quality franchise. Anyone who joins the team should be able to follow the steps and achieve similar results if done right. You can't rely on memory, intuition, or individual talent. You need an operations manual, just as if you were setting up a performance factory.

Now, scaling also means automation. The more you can delegate to systems, the more time you'll have to think strategically. This doesn't mean you stop having humans trading, but rather using technology to support their decisions, filter opportunities, generate alerts, execute orders quickly, and review statistics. Automation allows your traders to focus on what's important and not waste time doing repetitive tasks. It also reduces human error, which is key when you manage larger capitals.

A crucial point in scalability is risk management. You can't operate with the same mindset when you manage $10,000 as when you manage $10 million. Greater capital means greater market exposure, and also greater pressure. You must have clear rules about how much capital is allocated to each strategy, how it's distributed among traders, what daily or weekly limits exist, and what to do in crisis scenarios. Scaling without tight risk control is like building a tall building on sand. Sooner or later, it will fall.

Another key aspect is diversification. When you scale, you need to protect your operations from becoming dependent on a single market, a single strategy, or a single star trader. That's why it's advisable to develop multiple trading systems, in different assets, and with different time frames. Have traders specialized in different areas. Don't let everything depend on the performance of gold or the euro. Diversification not only protects you, it also gives you more income opportunities and greater income stability.

You must also learn to scale talent. The team that took you to your current level won't always be the same one that takes you to the next. That doesn't mean you should replace anyone, but rather that you should incorporate more strategic profiles, with a business mindset, long-term vision, and experience managing larger structures. Perhaps you need a COO to help you manage daily operations, or a CFO to organize your internal finances. Perhaps it's time to hire a performance psychologist, a high-level programmer, or someone with an expert in legal compliance. Scaling isn't just about growing in traders; it's about growing in organizational intelligence.

Furthermore, scaling means attracting external capital. Many teams reach a point where they want to manage third-party money, whether through managed accounts, private funds, or institutional contracts. But to do it well, you need audit processes, full transparency, clear metrics, and a trusted brand. No one will give you their money just because you're profitable. They'll give it to you because they trust your system, your people, and your risk management. Therefore, part of growth also involves investing in your reputation, your professional presentation, your legality, and your administrative structure.

Along the same lines, it's common for operations to be divided into departments or functional areas. It's no longer just the trading team. There's also the educational team, if you decide to train new traders. The technology development team, if you want to create internal tools. The commercial area, if you decide to seek external capital. The support department, to serve your own clients or investors. Each of these areas requires managers, processes, metrics, and monitoring. In other words, it becomes a company.

And of course, you can't scale without a strong culture. When there are only a few people, culture is passed on naturally. But when the team grows, when new hires are constantly coming in, you need the culture to be defined, communicated, and protected. Everyone must understand the values that guide decisions, how a professional trader behaves within the team, what attitudes are not tolerated, and what principles are sacred. Culture is the glue that holds a scaling operation together. If it's lost, everything else falls apart.

Scaling your operation isn't a matter of luck or improvisation. It's a conscious, methodical, and often challenging process. It means moving from being an operator to becoming a builder. Moving from looking only at charts to looking at processes, people, systems, and big numbers. But if you do it right, the potential is immense. You won't just have a profitable business. You'll have an institutional firm that can grow without limits, train others, attract global capital, and make its mark on the trading world. That's the real game. The one for those who no longer operate alone, but who think big and act accordingly.

Founding Your Own Trading Agency

Founding your own trading agency is the most ambitious and transformative step you can take as an institutional trader. It's no longer just about trading well or having a profitable team. It's about creating a business structure capable of training new traders, managing external capital, and building a solid brand in the financial world. This step requires a broader vision, where trading remains the core, but business strategy, culture, branding, and scalability become equally important. You no longer think like an operator, you think like a founder.

The first step in founding your agency is to understand what type of agency you want to build. There are many ways to approach it. You can have an agency that trains traders from scratch and then integrates them into your own internal fund. You can have an agency that simply trains people in exchange for a tuition or subscription. You can have a mixed structure where you educate, operate internal capital, and also manage external client accounts. You can focus solely on algorithms, solely on discretionary trading, or a combination of both. The important thing is to be clear about your business model from the beginning, because it will define your future decisions, your internal structure, and even the profile of the team you'll need.

Once you've defined your model, you must address the legal aspects. This step can't be improvised. It's not about opening just any company, but one that will involve money, investments, people, training, and possibly financial regulation. Ideally, you should seek advice from lawyers with experience in fintech, investments, and financial structures. You'll need to legally incorporate your company, register your trademark, clearly define your terms and conditions, have formal contracts with traders, investors if there are any, and with the clients who participate in your training. You must also comply with the regulations of the country from which you operate and, if you're managing third-party funds, seriously analyze whether you need a license, regulation, or to operate under a legal framework that allows you to do so.

Technological infrastructure is another critical point. A trading agency cannot work with home-grown systems or improvised solutions. You must have robust servers, secure platforms, performance analysis systems, professional access to market data, backtesting tools if you use algorithms, and well-defined internal communication systems. Technology is an essential part of the service you offer. If it doesn't work accurately, if there are outages, delays, or errors, your credibility will be affected. This also means having reliable, in-house or outsourced technical support that can respond immediately to any incident.

In parallel, you must design your operational structure. Who is responsible for each area? Who is responsible for recruiting new traders? Who trains? Who evaluates results? Who manages investor relations if you decide to attract external capital? Who handles marketing, social media, and content? Founding an agency means that many tasks aren't related to operations, but rather to making the operation work. You'll need people who think about organization, processes, administration, and expansion.

This involves delegating, trusting, structuring functional hierarchies, and making decisions like a true entrepreneur.

One of the central pillars of your agency should be training. This isn't about promising that anyone will become a millionaire, but rather about building a real, demanding, and clear educational system with verifiable results. You can create an internal academy that trains traders from scratch and takes them through different stages, from the most basic theory to supervised practice in funded accounts. The goal is to be able to replicate talent, standardize mindsets, and maintain quality control over who joins the team. Training is also a business model in itself, but only if it's done well, responsibly, and ethically.

Another vital factor is company culture. From day one, you must define your agency's values, its guiding principles, the way decisions are made, and the type of people you want to attract. This is reflected in everything from the way you write your emails to how you respond to a crisis. An agency without culture is a disorganized agency, with constant turnover, lacking cohesion or identity. An agency with a strong culture, on the other hand, has a contagious energy, attracts quality talent, and generates long-term loyalty.

Personal or institutional branding will also play a key role. Founding an agency requires visibility. You need a social media presence, valuable content, documented success stories, positive reviews, and real testimonials. Your name and that of your agency must inspire trust. You must sound professional, confident, and ethical. There's no room for empty promises or aggressive strategies. The market is full of noise. Your agency must stand out for its clarity, solidity, and honesty. To achieve this, you can build a content strategy, host conferences, educational videos, webinars, and all kinds of materials that position you as a leader in the industry.

Another important point will be your financing strategy. At first, you'll likely work with your own capital. But as you grow, you may need to raise external capital, fund more accounts, or even create a prop trading-type structure. This is where credibility comes in. If your results are solid and your structure is well-established, it won't be difficult to attract investors. But if there's disarray, a lack of transparency, or unrealistic promises, you'll close more doors than you open. Every step you take in this regard should be documented, audited, and backed by data.

Finally, founding an agency is also about thinking long-term. You're not creating something for a month or a year. You're building an organization that can outlive you. An agency with processes so well-crafted that it can grow with new leaders, new traders, and new markets. A structure capable of withstanding crises, adapting to technological change, and scaling without losing its essence. This kind of mindset requires patience, vision, and a true commitment to excellence.

Founding your own trading agency is a huge step, but also one of the most rewarding experiences a trader with an institutional vision can have. You don't just trade. You build. You don't just win. You leave a legacy.

And you do it with knowledge, structure, people, and purpose. That's the difference between an ordinary trader and a true architect of the financial world.

Attract and Train New Traders for your Agency

Recruiting and training new traders for your agency is one of the most important, delicate, and strategic tasks you'll have as the leader of an institutional project. You're not just looking for people who want to learn; you're looking for talent that can become part of your growth engine. Every trader who joins your agency represents an investment of time, energy, money, and attention. If you choose well, you can build a profitable, disciplined, and reliable team. If you choose poorly, you can lose valuable resources, affect internal morale, and even tarnish your agency's reputation. That's why this process must be well thought out, well structured, and executed with judgment and a long-term vision.

The first step is recruitment. And this is where many agencies fail. Some believe that attracting people is simply a matter of placing ads on social media or launching aggressive advertising campaigns. But it's not just about attracting attention; it's about attracting the right profile. What you're looking for isn't simply quantity, but quality. Committed people with a strong mindset, a capacity for learning, emotional self-control, and, above all, a hunger for real growth. People who want to be part of something bigger than themselves. To achieve this, you need to build a brand that clearly communicates your philosophy. Your content, your publications, your videos, your interviews—everything you do should make clear the type of agency you lead and the type of traders you want to develop. You're not offering promises of easy money; you're offering a serious path for those who want to become trading professionals.

Once you've captured the attention of potential candidates, you must have an intelligent selection process. You can use forms with questions that reveal their way of thinking, interviews to assess their trading vision, tests to understand their psychological profile, and dynamics that show you if they're truly willing to undergo a rigorous training process. The important thing is to filter. Don't be afraid to exclude those who don't fit your vision. The more refined your filter, the more solid your foundation will be. This also raises the prestige of your agency: when people know that not just anyone can get in, they begin to value what you offer much more.

Then comes the training process, and here you need a system. A true educational system, not just a series of videos or single classes. You must design a training path in stages, where each phase prepares the trader for the next. You can divide it, for example, into a theoretical phase, a practical demo phase, a supervised real-life practice phase, and finally, the integration phase into the trading team. Each of these phases must have clear objectives, evaluation metrics, real-life exercises, and personalized support. It's not just about teaching technique, but also about developing mindset, habits, and emotional control. An institutional trader doesn't just need to know how to enter and exit a trade. They need to learn to stay calm, follow the plan, obey rules, and adapt to new market conditions.

It's also important that the training is based on your own trading models. Don't teach a thousand different strategies. Teach the ones you and your team actually use. The ones that have been proven to work, the ones that make sense, the ones you can explain clearly. A new trader needs structure, a concrete framework, not a range of contradictory theories. This doesn't mean limiting their creativity; it means giving them a solid foundation on which to build their style over time.

Another key point in training is practice. A trader isn't trained on theory alone. They need to trade, make mistakes, receive feedback, and try again. That's why it's a good idea to include live simulations, daily trade reviews, group sessions, and personalized mentoring. You can even establish a mentoring system, where more advanced traders guide newer traders through their growth process. This strengthens the internal culture and accelerates learning. It's also recommended that you teach them from the start how to keep logs, record their trades, analyze their mistakes, and establish a daily routine. These are the tools that generate the most value in the long term.

During the training process, you should also be observing other aspects that don't appear in the graphs. Their attitude, their level of commitment, how they react to frustration, whether they complain or learn, whether they follow instructions or look for shortcuts. All of this will give you clear signals about who has potential and who doesn't. Not everyone who enters will make it to the end, and that's okay. Your system should have filters at every stage. This way, you ensure that only the most committed and consistent people make it to operating real accounts or becoming part of your institutional team.

Once training is complete, you can make several decisions. If the trader has demonstrated proficiency, you can offer them the opportunity to operate an account funded with agency capital. You can integrate them into a team. You can offer them the role of trainer for new traders or even invite them to participate in expansion projects. You can also open the option of managing external capital if your agency allows it. The important thing is that the traders who are part of your agency feel there is a real path to growth. That they weren't just trained and then released, but now belong to something. This generates loyalty, motivation, and a sense of purpose.

Finally, it's important to continue training your team, even after you've brought them on board. Learning never stops in the trading world. There are always new tools, new market conditions, and new strategies to refine. You can organize internal bootcamps, refresher sessions, monthly performance reviews, and intensive training sessions. You can also invite external experts or experienced traders to share their experience. All of this keeps the spirit of learning alive and prevents the agency from stagnating.

Attracting and training new traders isn't a secondary task. It's the heart of your agency. It's the process that ensures your vision expands, your team grows, and your brand strengthens. Do it intelligently, seriously, and with passion. You'll see that there's no greater satisfaction than seeing someone who started from scratch in your system become a profitable, professional trader who's proud to be part of your project. That's creating a legacy. That's building a true institutional trading empire.

Monetize Talent

Monetizing talent within an institutional trading agency is one of the most powerful and profitable ideas you can implement if you truly want your company to scale and become a solid source of income. Talent is not only valuable for what it produces in terms of trades, but also for its ability to generate new lines of business, inspire others, and multiply the impact of your vision. A talented trader not only makes money from their own trades, but can also generate income for you and the agency in multiple ways if you know how to channel their potential intelligently and structuredly.

The first step to monetizing talent is recognizing it early. Within your team, there will always be people who stand out. Some will have a very precise technical approach, others will master market psychology, and still others will have a natural charisma that makes them good leaders or communicators. Your task is to identify each team member's strength. Not all should be the same, but all should add value. The common mistake many agencies make is to treat all their traders as interchangeable parts. But if you manage to recognize the unique talent in each one and give them room to grow, that person can become an additional source of income, even beyond their market performance.

A direct and clear way to monetize talent is through funding. If you have profitable traders, you can assign them larger accounts and keep a percentage of their profits. This seems simple, but it's extremely powerful. The more talent you develop and the more accounts you operate under your structure, the more money flows into the agency without you having to operate directly. You're monetizing the skills of others, but in a fair and collaborative way. They win, you win, the agency grows. This model can also be applied with external capital, where you manage accounts for institutional clients or private funds and put your best talent in charge of those operations.

Another way to monetize talent is to turn your best traders into trainers. Not every good trader knows how to teach, but some do. You can offer advanced training programs where these traders share their method, experience, and way of thinking with newcomers. These courses can be in-person, virtual, or even through a membership model. The key is to package real, proven knowledge and turn it into a profitable training product. When someone pays to learn from a trader who's already winning, they do so with much more confidence and willingness. Furthermore, this type of in-house training allows you to scale without losing quality, because you're teaching exactly what already works within your own structure.

You can also monetize talent through content. Some traders have a natural ability to communicate, create videos, and explain complex concepts in a simple way. If you identify someone like this, you can support them in building a digital presence that benefits the agency. They can create YouTube channels, podcasts, articles, and live streams. All of this not only builds authority for your brand but can also become a channel for attracting new traders, new investors, or new students. You can even monetize these channels directly through advertising, sponsorships, or digital products. A talented trader in front of a camera can generate as much money as trading in the markets, if you know how to structure the strategy well.

Another more advanced option is to convert talent into technology. If you have traders with programming, data analysis, or automation skills, you can create algorithmic models based on their strategies. These bots or automated systems can be sold, licensed, or used to operate larger accounts without relying on the human factor. This turns knowledge into digital assets that generate more scalable revenue. You can even sell indicators, analytical tools, or management platforms developed within your agency. When talent produces something useful and replicable, you have a gold mine on your hands.

Additionally, you can explore strategic alliances. If you have traders who excel in certain market niches, such as futures, stocks, forex, or cryptocurrencies, you can partner with brokers, platforms, or funds interested in that type of trading. Talent then becomes a calling card for special conditions, shared commissions, or joint projects. These alliances not only bring in money, they also better position you in the financial ecosystem. Your agency's reputation grows as your traders excel in different fields.

Another idea is to open internal lines of specialization. For example, if one of your traders becomes an expert in macroeconomic analysis, you can offer premium reports to institutional clients. If another specializes in scalping, they can lead a live trading room. If you have someone with coaching skills, they can offer one-on-one sessions for external traders. In this way, you turn each member of your team into a micro-business within the agency, with products or services that generate additional income. This approach breaks with the traditional model of having employees operating accounts and nothing more. You begin to see them as strategic partners, as key pieces of a larger structure.

Of course, all of this requires organization, clear contracts, fair profit sharing, and a well-defined culture of meritocracy. It's not about exploiting your team, but rather offering them real opportunities to grow, earn more, and feel part of something bigger. The more space you give them to monetize their talents, the more committed they'll be to the agency's success. And the most interesting thing is that this creates a virtuous cycle: you attract better talent, develop it, monetize it, reinvest in the agency, grow, and the cycle repeats itself on a larger scale.

Monetizing talent is a skill of vision. It means seeing beyond daily operations and understanding that each trader is a developing asset. If you know how to cultivate their skills, offer them growth paths, and connect them with real opportunities, you can turn your agency into a value-generating machine. Not just a company that makes money, but a structure that multiplies the impact of knowledge, experience, and discipline. That is the essence of intelligent institutional trading: building an ecosystem where talent flows, is empowered, and generates wealth for everyone involved.

Marketing for Trading Agencies

Marketing for trading agencies is one of the fundamental pillars if you want to scale, attract top talent, secure investors, and build a respected brand in the financial world. You can have the best team, the best results, and a solid strategy, but if no one knows you exist, you simply won't grow. Marketing isn't an option; it's a necessity if you're building a serious agency. And most importantly, it's not just about creating buzz, but about communicating authority, professionalism, and real results. People interested in trading don't want empty promises; they want proof, transparency, and a clear identity.

The first step to a good marketing strategy is defining your positioning. What type of agency are you? Who are you targeting? Are you a firm that trains traders from scratch or do you seek out already-trained talent? Do you focus on institutional clients or retail traders? Are you an aggressive, young brand, or a traditional, serious firm? All of this matters because every marketing decision must revolve around that positioning. You can't communicate the same way with a 20-year-old who wants to learn how to scalp as you can with an investment fund looking for capital management. Therefore, before spending a single cent on advertising or opening a social media account, you need to be clear about what type of agency you are and what type of ideal client you want to attract.

Next comes your digital presence. In today's age, if you're not online, you don't exist. Your agency must have a professional, clear, functional, and visually appealing website. No buggy pages, decade-old designs, or vague information. Your website should show who you are, what you do, your results, how you can work with them, and why someone should trust you. Include testimonials, audited statistics, team profiles, and simple calls to action. It's not about having an online encyclopedia, but about anyone arriving at your agency understanding in a minute that they're dealing with a serious and professional firm.

Then there's the content. This is where you can really stand out and attract people organically. If you want traders to find you, investors to take you seriously, and others to recommend you, you have to share valuable knowledge. This can take many forms: explanatory videos on YouTube, market analysis on LinkedIn, articles on your blog, podcasts, free reports, or live streams showcasing the team's operations. Content should be educational, real, and consistent with your brand. If your agency is technical and professional, don't publish memes or empty promises. If it's young and modern, don't use rigid and distant language. Content should educate, engage, and build trust.

One channel that tends to work very well in this sector is YouTube. If any of your traders have a strong on-camera presence, you can create a series of videos where they explain analysis, share strategies, answer frequently asked questions, or simply show the day-to-day life inside the agency. These videos are highly positioned in the long term and allow you to connect with audiences who will later become students, traders, or partners. You don't need millions of views; you just need to connect with the right people. And if you're consistent, that community will gradually grow organically.

You should also have an active presence on social media, especially those that focus on the financial world. LinkedIn is excellent for connecting with professionals, investors, and other key players in the ecosystem. Instagram works well for showcasing the human side of the team, achievements, the work environment, and events. Twitter (now X) is useful for quick market commentary or sparking debate. And TikTok, although it seems more informal, is increasingly attracting more young profiles interested in learning about investments and finance. The trick is to tailor your message to each network. Don't post the same thing everywhere. On LinkedIn, talk about results and structure. On Instagram, show the process and your day-to-day life. On TikTok, simplify complex concepts in creative ways. Each network is a different tool.

Don't underestimate the power of email marketing either. When someone gives you their email address in exchange for a free resource, such as an ebook, class, report, or tool, they're giving you permission to speak to them directly. Take advantage of this channel to send valuable content, agency updates, opportunities to join your team, or new product launches. Email remains one of the most effective and profitable ways to convert audiences into clients or collaborators. Don't use it just to sell, though. Use email to educate, connect, and build relationships.

If you have the budget, you can invest in paid advertising. Platforms like Meta Ads, Google Ads, or even TikTok Ads can be very useful for attracting qualified traffic to your website or a landing page. But don't launch campaigns without a strategy. First, make sure everything else is in place: your message, your brand, your content, your funnel. Advertising doesn't fix a bad product; it just exposes it faster. When you invest, do so with clear objectives: capture leads, generate signups, position your brand. And measure everything. Digital marketing can be adjusted and optimized, but only if you know what's working and what isn't.

Another important aspect is networking. Your agency should be present at events, conferences, trade shows, and meetings in the financial sector. Attending these events allows you to connect with other professionals, find alliances, showcase your brand, and open doors to collaborations or funding. You can also organize your own events: webinars, bootcamps, masterclasses, even internal trading competitions. All of this builds community and reinforces your authority. When people see that you're active, that you share value, and that you're truly committed to the industry, they perceive you as trustworthy and relevant.

Finally, take care of your reputation. The trading world is full of false promises, fraud, and smoke and mirrors. Don't fall for that game. You don't need to exaggerate to sell. Good results, professionalism, and time speak for themselves. If you promise impossible things or use manipulative marketing techniques, sooner or later it will come back to haunt you. Be transparent, show both your successes and your mistakes, and always maintain clear ethics. That will give you something much more valuable than virality: it will give you credibility.

Marketing for trading agencies isn't about looking big, it's about being big and then communicating it well. If you have a clear vision, a committed team, and a solid structure, marketing will be the tool that allows you to scale, attract opportunities, and build a brand that lasts. Don't put it off. Marketing is part of the business. It's what connects your work to the world. And if you do it right, it can be the reason your agency goes from being a good team to becoming a benchmark in the industry.

Creating a Respected Brand in the Industry

Creating a respected brand in the trading industry doesn't happen by accident. It's not built overnight, nor simply because you make money trading. A respected brand is born from a combination of real results, solid values, consistency in messaging, and, above all, a deep respect for those who follow you, watch you, or want to work with you. When we talk about branding, we're not just talking about a pretty logo or a catchy name. We're talking about what others say about you when you're not there. We're talking about reputation. About trust. About what you stand for. And in a world like trading, where empty promises and fakers abound, building that reputation is a challenge... but also a great opportunity.

The first pillar of building a respected brand is transparency. If your agency operates honestly, shows real results, acknowledges mistakes, and has a clear communication policy, you'll quickly stand out from the crowd. Many in this industry thrive on hype. They inflate their performance, hide their losses, and edit their statistics. And at first, it may seem like they're gaining attention, but in the long run, that backfires. A brand that aspires to be respected must choose the difficult path: always telling the truth, even when it's inconvenient. Because that honesty, when maintained over time, builds something much more powerful than a quick return. It builds credibility.

The second pillar is consistency. Your brand can't say one thing and do another. If you talk about discipline on your social media, but then your team behaves arrogantly or unethically, you're breaking your own narrative. If you preach about financial education but sell empty courses and promises of getting rich in three days, your message becomes noise. Consistency is reflected in everything: in what you post, in how you speak, in how you treat your clients, in the environment you create within your agency, and even in how you make difficult decisions. A respected brand is consistent because people need to know they can trust what it stands for, not just what it promises.

The third pillar is quality. Everything that comes out of your agency, whether it's a course, a video, a presentation, a webinar, or a mentoring session, must be well-made. It doesn't need to be perfect, but it must be professional. Paying attention to detail communicates respect for your audience. If you upload content, make sure it's well-edited. If you host events, make sure they're well-organized. If you teach a class, make sure it's well-structured. Don't underestimate what quality conveys. A brand that cares about what it offers demonstrates that it values those who receive it. Mediocrity is the worst enemy of respect. And in such a competitive industry, quality is a powerful differentiator.

Another crucial factor is impact. Brands that are truly respected in the industry don't just make money, they generate value for others. They teach, inspire, elevate the conversation. They train new traders, improve the ecosystem, and create opportunities for others. If your agency becomes a space where people improve, grow, find direction, and gain real tools, you will inevitably gain respect. A powerful brand isn't one that imposes itself, but one that becomes necessary. And to be necessary, you have to contribute something that positively transforms the lives or work of those around you.

Long-term consistency is also key. You can have a great campaign, a viral video, or an amazing month, but if that doesn't sustain itself, your brand will fall flat. What truly builds a strong reputation is the constant repetition of good decisions, good content, good results, and good customer service. People don't remember what you did once, but what you do consistently. That's why building a respected brand isn't a sprint; it's a marathon. Every action counts. Every word counts. Every interaction leaves a mark. And the more time you spend doing things right, the stronger that mark will be.

It's also important to define a clear identity. What is your brand voice? Are you technical and serious? Friendly and educational? Disruptive and innovative? Whatever your style, it must be authentic. The most respected brands don't copy others; they're built from within. If you and your team have your own personality, if you speak from experience, if you communicate with truth and passion, it shows. People don't connect with the generic; they connect with the genuine. And when your identity is clear, you naturally begin to attract the right people: clients who value your approach, traders who share your vision, investors who trust your judgment.

A much-overlooked but extremely important aspect is how you handle conflict. Sooner or later, you'll encounter a complaint, a criticism, a public mistake, or an awkward situation. How you respond to it defines much of your brand. If you hide, attack, or deny responsibility, you lose credibility. But if you face it with humility, provide clear explanations, and take corrective action, your reputation grows. Truly respected brands aren't those that never fail, but those that know how to bounce back with class and responsibility. Respect is earned especially in difficult times.

Furthermore, if you really want to establish yourself, surrounding yourself with other respected brands is a great strategy. Alliances, collaborations, and partnerships with reputable individuals or companies automatically elevate you. It's not about using others as ladders, but rather about joining forces, sharing a vision, and building together. If you're serious, you'll attract serious people. And that quality network, over time, becomes its own ecosystem where trust flows, projects multiply, and respect is reinforced.

Finally, remember that your brand isn't just external; it's also internal. What your team says about you, how they feel about working with you, how they talk about the agency when they're not in the office—all of that is also part of your brand. If you want to be respected by the market, start by being respected by your people. Create an environment where your values are lived, where there are real opportunities for growth, where treatment is fair, and decisions are consistent. Internal culture is the most authentic reflection of a brand. And if that culture is strong, everything else is built on a firm foundation.

Creating a respected brand in the trading industry is a constant mission. It's not bought, copied, or faked. It's built with every decision, every word, every action. And if you do it right, you won't just attract clients or traders, you'll attract something more important: admiration. Because a brand that earns respect not only survives over time, but also becomes a benchmark. And when your agency is seen as an example, you'll know you've done something much bigger than just making money. You've left your mark.

Automation and Technology to Scale Without Limits

In the world of institutional trading, there comes a time when you can no longer do everything alone. Even a small team can't handle everything when trading volume, the number of traders, administrative tasks, and growth demands multiply. This is where automation and technology become your greatest allies. We're not talking about a luxury or a fad; we're talking about a real necessity if your goal is to scale without limits. Automation is what allows you to do more with less effort, reduce human error, make faster decisions, and free up valuable time that can be used to think strategically instead of putting out daily fires.

Let's take it step by step. The first thing you need to understand is that automation isn't the same as becoming a robot. Nor does it mean letting machines control everything. Automation is simply building intelligent systems that handle repetitive, technical, or low-emotional tasks so you and your team can focus on what's important: analyzing, deciding, leading, and growing. In a trading agency, there are many areas that can be effectively automated. For example, entering and exiting trades based on defined parameters, managing risk by account or trader, verifying compliance with certain internal rules, distributing reports, and tracking performance metrics.

One of the most important steps is investing in a solid technological infrastructure from the start. This includes secure servers, fast connections, management software, and advanced trading platforms. But it's not just about purchasing technology; it's about using it strategically. If you have a system that can detect behavioral patterns among your traders, then you can see who is risking more than they can afford or who is repeating mistakes. If you integrate automated dashboards that update in real time, you can make faster management decisions. And if you develop your own tools, you can offer unique and customized services that differentiate you from other agencies.

Technology also allows you to scale without losing control. You can have 100 traders operating simultaneously in different parts of the world and still have a central system overseeing everything. This is impossible if you rely solely on humans. Automation gives you eyes everywhere, alerts you to deviations, and can even stop trades that put capital at risk before they turn into big losses. Imagine having a system that, as soon as it detects that a trader has exceeded their daily loss limit, automatically closes their positions and locks them out for the day. This not only protects your money, but also gives you peace of mind as the operation leader.

Another important part of automation is training. You can use technology to teach more effectively and without taking up all your time. E-learning platforms, pre-recorded classes, market simulators, automated feedback, and interactive quizzes are all tools you can use to train new traders while you focus on expanding your operation. You can even create a system that evaluates each trader's progress and classifies them by level, assigning them a mentor or strategy type based on their strengths and weaknesses. This way, your training process becomes more precise, more efficient, and, most importantly, more scalable.

The next logical step in this path is developing algorithms. When I talk about algorithms, I don't necessarily mean trading robots that operate completely autonomously for you. I'm referring to semi-automated systems that help your traders make better decisions. For example, alerts that are triggered when certain market conditions are met, tools that analyze in seconds what would take a human hours, or models that suggest possible entries based on historical patterns. These systems can be developed by your internal team or by external programmers under your supervision. The important thing is that they respond to a real need and integrate well with your business model.

One of the biggest advantages of automation is that it reduces emotional errors. Humans make mistakes due to fatigue, anxiety, or simply distraction. Automated systems, on the other hand, do exactly what they were programmed to do, without stress or hesitation. This gives you consistency, which is very valuable when you handle large volumes. It also allows you to standardize the experience for all your traders. If everyone trades with the same type of technological assistance, the results become more predictable, easier to analyze, and simpler to scale.

But of course, not everything is rosy. Automation requires investment: time, money, and knowledge. You also need security, because any technological gap can be costly. That's why, from the beginning, you should work with trusted programmers, recognized suppliers, and systems with technical support. Don't rush into automation for the sake of automation. Start with the simplest and most impactful options. Then work your way up. The key is to first identify which tasks take up your time, which are repetitive, and which could be better done by a machine. And then build on that, specific, not generic, solutions.

A common misconception is that automation removes the human touch. Nothing could be further from the truth. Automation well gives you more space to be human. To lead, to converse with your traders, to inspire your team. You let technology do the hard work, so you can focus on what no machine can do: creating vision, making strategic decisions, motivating people, and building lasting relationships. The more you automate, the more time you have to think bigger.

Plus, technology allows you to internationalize your operation. You can work with people from anywhere in the world, regardless of time zone. Your platforms can work in different languages. You can use communication tools like Slack, Discord, or Zoom to keep your entire team connected. You can receive applications, conduct interviews, train new traders, and oversee operations, all from a virtual office. And when your operation goes digital, it also becomes scalable without borders.

Finally, remember that technology advances every day. What's cutting-edge today will be basic tomorrow. So your agency must stay constantly evolving. Regularly review what you can improve, what can be automated, and what new tools have come onto the market. Attend tech conferences, talk to other leaders, and invest in innovation. Because if you stand still, technology won't wait for you. But if you use it well, it becomes your most powerful advantage.

Scaling without limits isn't a fantasy. It's a reality that's already happening. And it's happening thanks to automation and technology. You decide whether you want to be one of those who watch others grow exponentially, or one of those who lead that transformation. In a business where time is precious and mistakes cost thousands, automation is more than just a good idea. It's the smartest path to operational freedom and sustained growth.

Your Legacy as an Institutional Trading Leader

Becoming a leader in the world of institutional trading is a path that requires vision, tireless work, discipline, and a different mindset. But when you finally get there, there's something that starts to weigh more than money, more than numbers or personal achievements. It's the legacy you'll leave behind. Because everything you build, everything you train, everything you teach, everything you inspire in others is what truly transcends. Legacy isn't measured in bank accounts, but in the mark you leave on people, on the industry, and on the generations of traders who will come after you.

Many leaders in the trading world focus solely on making money, and that's fine, because that's part of the game. But true leaders look beyond. They want to build something that lasts, something that continues to grow even when they're no longer sitting in front of their screens. And to do that, it's essential to change the way you view your role within your agency, within the market, and within the professional trading ecosystem.

Leaving a legacy starts with the people. The people you trained, guided, and inspired. The trader you gave their first opportunity. The analyst who started from scratch with you and ended up leading teams. The insecure young man who became a disciplined trader thanks to your trust and your teachings. A true legacy is built on every conversation in which you offered direction, every mistake you patiently corrected, and every example you set with your own behavior. Because your daily actions, whether you realize it or not, are what set the standard for others.

Your legacy is also built on your vision. The rules, values, and principles you decided to operate your agency with. If you chose transparency over greed. If you prioritized education over idle speculation. If you created a culture of discipline, accountability, and constant improvement, that's what others will remember and what will influence the decisions others make when it's their turn to lead. Because leaders inspire with what they do more than what they say. And if your values were strong, your team's values will likely be strong too, even many years after you've retired or changed roles.

Another way to leave a legacy is by professionalizing the profession. Institutional trading still has a long way to go in many countries. There's still a lot of myth, a lot of informality, a lot of confusion. If you build a reputable agency, with clear processes, respect for regulations, solid training, and auditable results, you're raising the bar for the entire industry. And that not only positions you as a benchmark, but also opens doors for others. You're helping more people approach trading as a real career, not a passing experiment. And the evolution you manage to foster around you is an essential part of your legacy.

We also can't ignore that a legacy is built on the information you share. Many leaders keep what they know to themselves for fear of others surpassing them. But true leaders teach fearlessly. They hold nothing back. They understand that knowledge is only valuable if it's passed on. When you train traders who later surpass your results, when your method becomes the basis for other agencies, when your teachings end up improving the lives of people you don't even know, that's when you know you're building something great. It doesn't matter if you write books, give lectures, or simply train your team day after day with discipline and clarity. Every little bit counts.

There's a very important point that also defines your legacy: how you handled difficult times. Because every team, every agency, every leader goes through dark times. Losses, mistakes, betrayals, crises. But what determines your legacy isn't avoiding those moments, but how you faced them. Whether you acted calmly, honestly, responsibly. Whether you cared for your people instead of blaming them. Whether you rebuilt intelligently instead of giving up. All of this leaves a deep mark on those who follow you. And those who were there with you will never forget.

Now, when we talk about legacy, we're also talking about sustainability. Not just about what you achieve today, but about what will continue to work when you're no longer leading. Therefore, a true legacy involves creating systems that work without you. Developing leaders within your agency. Creating documented processes. Developing an autonomous culture, where values are maintained even if you're silent. If your team only functions well when you're in charge, then you don't have a legacy; you have a dependency. But if your team continues to grow, continues to operate, continues to improve without the need for your constant supervision, then you've built something that can last for decades.

A legacy also extends outward. If your agency helps the community, sponsors training programs for talented young people, supports financial inclusion initiatives, or creates quality free content, you're leaving a mark far beyond trading. You're using your success to improve the environment. You're contributing to a fairer, more professional, more accessible economy. That's true leadership. That's legacy.

Ultimately, your legacy is personal. It doesn't have to be gigantic to be valuable. You might not have founded the largest agency in the world, but if you changed the lives of a handful of traders, if you created a dignified and respectful work environment, if you taught with passion, if you lived your principles until your very last day, then your legacy is real, profound, and powerful. Because in the end, every leader leaves. The question is what remains when you leave. What ideas, what customs, what culture, what memories, and what inspiration remain.

That's your legacy. And you're writing it every day, whether you realize it or not. Every decision, every word, every action adds or subtracts. So the best time to start building it with intention is now. Leading in institutional trading is a privilege. But leaving a legacy is an honor. A gift you give to the world that no one can take away from you.

www.ingramcontent.com/pod-product-compliance
Lightning Source LLC
LaVergne TN
LVHW090417210926
848480LV00002B/602
* 9 7 9 8 2 3 1 1 7 0 1 8 0 *